DINKY
DAISY,

Published by World International Publishing Limited
under the Young Wordsworth imprint.
All rights reserved.
Copyright © 1993 World International Publishing Limited,
an Egmont Company, Egmont House, PO Box 111,
Great Ducie Street, Manchester M60 3BL.
Printed in Hungary.
ISBN 0 7498 1658 9

The Magical Storybook

written and illustrated by
Gill Guile

CONTENTS

Andrew and Jane go on a journey
into the world of nursery rhymes.
They meet Jack and Jill, Humpty Dumpty
and lots of other favourites inside the pages of ...

THE ENCHANTED BOOK

Andrew yawned loudly and looked at Jane, who was already fast asleep.

"I think it's time you went to sleep," said Mummy, as she put down the nursery rhyme book that she had been reading. She kissed the two children goodnight and tucked them in.

"Sweet dreams," whispered Mummy as she closed the door.

Andrew snuggled down in his bed and began
to doze. The moon shone brightly outside and,
through a gap in the curtains, a moonbeam fell
on the nursery rhyme book, which lay open on
Andrew's bed. The last thing he saw as he
drifted off to sleep was a picture of Jack and
Jill climbing up a large green hill . . .

Jack and Jill went up the hill
To fetch a pail of water.
Jack fell down and broke his crown,
And Jill came tumbling after.

Andrew and Jane woke to the sound of children's laughter. Jane rubbed her eyes in disbelief as she stared at the nursery rhyme book beside the bed. It was as big as a door and open at the Jack and Jill nursery rhyme!

Andrew took Jane's hand and pulled her towards the enormous book and, to their amazement, they passed straight through the pages and into the world of nursery rhymes.

14

In the distance they could see two children climbing a steep hill carrying an empty bucket between them.

"Why, it's Jack and Jill!" exclaimed Jane.

"We'd better tell them to be careful or they may fall and hurt themselves," said Andrew.

They hurried off towards the hill, but before they could get there Jack and Jill slipped in a puddle and tumbled down the hill with a great splash of water.

Jack and Jill were a little shaken, but not too badly hurt. Andrew and Jane bandaged their heads and warned them to take more care.

"Oh, don't worry," said Jack. "We fall down every day." And they picked up their empty bucket and started up the hill once again.

"Why don't you visit the Hey Diddle Diddle people in the next valley?" called Jack as he waved goodbye.

18

Hey diddle diddle,
The cat and the fiddle,
The cow jumped over the moon.
The little dog laughed
To see such fun,
And the dish ran away with the spoon.

As Andrew and Jane walked into the valley they heard a tune that the cat was playing on his fiddle. They skipped down the slope to meet the animals.

"Hello there," Andrew said loudly. But the cat simply bowed and played another tune, the dog laughed and rolled around on the grass, and the dish and the spoon ran away without a word!

"How peculiar!" said Andrew.

"The cow looks quite sensible, let's say hello to her," suggested Jane.

20

"I'm sorry, but I really can't stop and chat," said the cow. "I have to jump over the moon tonight, and it's already quite late. Would you like to come along for the ride? I could drop you off at Humpty Dumpty's wall."

"Ooh, yes please," said Andrew and Jane together, and they climbed on to the cow's back and off they went, right over the moon, with one enormous leap!

22

Humpty Dumpty sat on a wall.
Humpty Dumpty had a great fall.
All the King's horses and all the King's men
Couldn't put Humpty together again.

After a wonderful ride through the stars the cow landed beside a very high stone wall just as the sun was rising.

"Look up there!" cried Jane, pointing to a small figure perched on top of the wall.

It was Humpty Dumpty, and he was wobbling dangerously.

"I think we should go up and help him before he falls off," said Andrew.

They climbed the wooden ladder which was leaning against the wall and crawled along the top towards Humpty Dumpty.

24

Before they could reach him Humpty began to wobble even more, and suddenly he toppled right off the wall. He landed on the grass with a loud thump in front of some soldiers on horseback.

"They'll never patch him up," said Andrew.

"Poor Humpty!" cried Jane.

Then a sudden gust of wind caught them by surprise and swept *them* off the wall too.

Down and down they tumbled, head over heels, never seeming to get any nearer to the ground.

Then they dropped into a fluffy cloud and everything went dark.

Andrew hit the ground with a bump and opened his eyes. He was lying on the bedroom floor in a heap of rumpled sheets. In the next bed Jane was still fast asleep.

"It must have been a dream," Andrew whispered to his teddy bear as he climbed back into bed. Then he noticed the nursery rhyme book lying where Mummy had left it earlier that night.

"That's very strange," said Andrew. "Mummy left the book open at Jack and Jill, but now it's open at Humpty Dumpty! I can't wait to tell Jane tomorrow morning."

And he snuggled down to go to sleep once again.

30

Humpty Dumpty peeped out of the nursery rhyme book and waited until Andrew was fast asleep, then he quickly turned the pages back to Jack and Jill before disappearing back into the book once again.

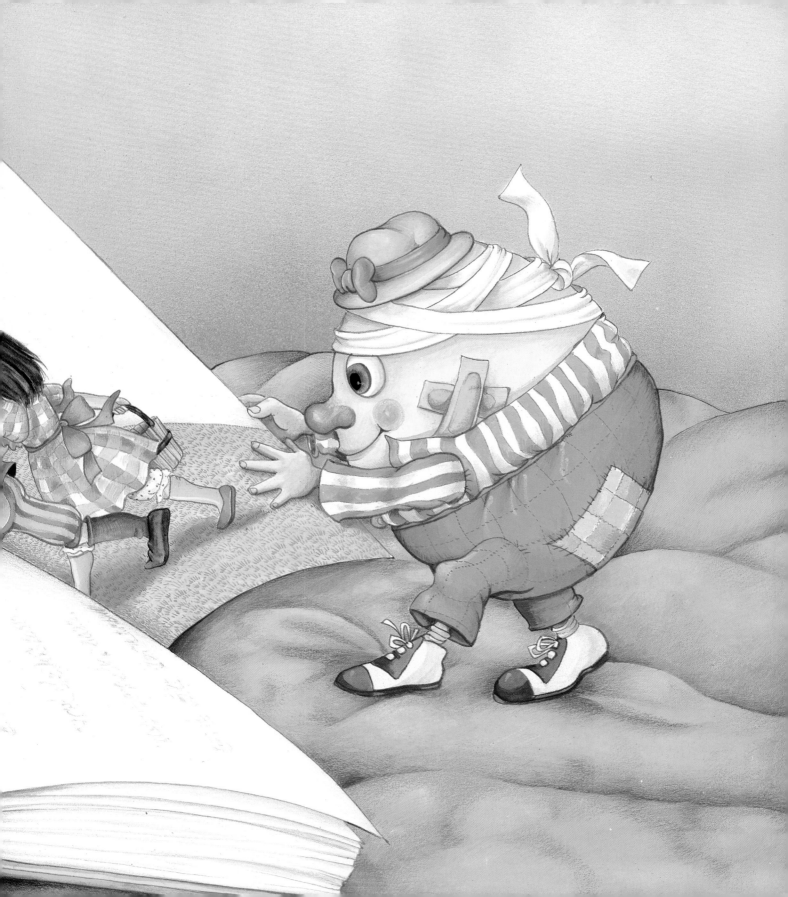

Jane and Andrew need some help
when Jane's doll gets broken.
They set off on a magical journey through Toyland
to find the Toymender when they get aboard ...

THE
MAGIC
TRAIN

The day began like any other day, with Andrew and Jane playing happily with their toys in the nursery. Then Jane accidentally dropped her doll and cracked its head.

Andrew tried to repair the damage with bandages and plasters, but he used so many that the doll's face was completely hidden beneath them!

They did not notice that behind them the nursery toys were coming to life . . .

Andrew and Jane looked at each other in astonishment. All the toys were as big as they were — or perhaps *they* were as small as the toys!

Before they could decide one way or the other, Andrew's teddy bear asked them to climb on to the toy train, with the injured doll, so that they could go to Toyland to see the Toymender. Their journey would take them through four very strange lands.

The train blew its whistle and puff-puffed its way out of the nursery and into the Land of Sweets, where everything could be eaten.

The train sped along a chocolate road surrounded by trees made from stripy seaside rock, topped with candyfloss, and passed fields of flowers made from a colourful assortment of humbugs and candy drops – all with sugared petals and minty leaves.

Teddy slowed the train down as they passed a river of lemonade and Andrew and Jane reached out and scooped handfuls of lemonade to drink. It tasted delicious.

Suddenly the train began to pick up speed. It went faster and faster, making Andrew and Jane cling to the sides of the train. Andrew asked Teddy why the train was going so fast.

Teddy told him that they were in the Land of the Goblins, and that if the goblins caught them they would keep them there forever.

Jane screamed as lots of ugly little men, waving large sticks, ran after the train. Teddy told them not to worry, and he drove even faster, leaving the angry goblins far, far behind.

44

Eventually they passed over a mountain
and into the Land of Upside Down,
where everything was the wrong way round.

Andrew and Jane giggled when they saw the
cows standing on their heads munching
daisies, and birds flying upside down in the
sky. Families of rabbits hopped about on their
heads and even the trees stood with their
roots pointing at the sky. It all made Andrew
feel quite dizzy.

Soon they passed through a tunnel and came out into the Land of Birds. It was a fabulous place, full of exotic birds of so many colours and sizes that it was like riding through a rainbow.

Teddy had to slow the train down to a snail's pace so that they didn't bump into the birds as they crowded around the train, whistling and twittering.

48

After Andrew and Jane had travelled through the Land of Birds, Teddy announced their arrival at Toyland.

The train stopped by a toy fort and they watched as a squad of soldiers marched by.

Jane tried to catch a pair of brightly coloured beach balls as they bounced down the road, but they were too fast for her.

There were toys everywhere.

A Jack-in-the-box waved at Teddy and told him the Toymender was expecting them.

A short way down the road was a curious little shop. Over the door was a sign which said TOYMENDER OF TOYLAND. Teddy led the way down to the shop.

The Toymender was a kindly old man with white hair and odd little spectacles perched on the end of his nose. He took the injured doll into his work room and in no time at all he had given her a brand new head. Jane was delighted.

The Toymender was happy to have helped the doll, but before Andrew and Jane left to go home he wanted them to visit the Toyland Hospital.

The hospital was full of toys who were ill. There was a teddy with only one ear, a train with no wheels, a rocking horse with no rockers and, to Andrew and Jane's surprise, a torn and tattered puppet with broken strings which Jane recognised immediately.

54

The puppet was an old toy which they had broken long ago. Andrew and Jane had put it away at the bottom of their toybox and forgotten all about it.

They were so sorry for neglecting the puppet that the Toymender said he would repair it if they promised to play with it every day so that it would never feel lonely again. They agreed at once.

56

Soon it was time to leave and they all climbed back on to the train and waved goodbye to the Toymender and all the toys.

The train sped along so quickly that everything became a blur of colour and Andrew and Jane began to feel sleepy. Soon they were fast asleep.

When Andrew and Jane woke up they were back in the nursery and the toys were scattered around the floor — just as they had left them.

Andrew began to tidy his toys away, taking care not to damage them. He wondered if it had all been a dream, until he saw Jane staring at her doll, which had a beautiful new head.

Then they noticed their old puppet propped against the toy box. All its torn and tattered clothes had been cleaned and mended and it had a new set of strings. They decided it could not have been a dream after all, and when they looked at the puppet again — they saw it wink!

60